CW00323899

GARLANDS

GARLANDS

Techniques and Materials...Step-by-Step Projects...
Creative Ideas for the Year Round

by Richard Kollath
Photography by Robert Hoebermann

Facts On File Publications
OXFORD•NEW YORK

A FRIEDMAN GROUP BOOK

Copyright © 1988 by Michael Friedman Publishing Group, Inc.

All rights reserved. No part of this publication may be reproduced, stored in a retrieval system, or transmitted, in any form or by any means, electronic, mechanical, photocopying, recording, or otherwise, without the prior written permission of the publisher.

First published in 1988 by Facts On File Publications, Limited. Collins Street, Oxford, England OX4 1XJ

ISBN: 0-948894-25-3

GARLANDS: Techniques and Materials... Step-by-Step Projects... Creative Ideas For The Year Round
was prepared and produced by
Michael Friedman Publishing Group, Inc.
15 West 26th Street
New York, New York 10010

Editor: Tim Frew
Art Director/Designer: Mary Moriarty
Photo Editor: Christopher Bain
Production Manager: Karen L. Greenberg

Typeset by I, CLAVDIA, Inc.
Colour separations by Hong Kong Scanner Craft Company Ltd.
Printed and bound in Hong Kong by Leefung-Asco Printers Ltd.
1 2 3 4 5 6 7 8 9 10

Dedication

With great pride, I dedicate this book of garlands to my parents, who provided me with perpetual gardens, love, and encouragement. And to the memory of my Grandfather Richard.

Acknowledgments

This book of garlands has come about through the goodwill and talents of many friends and associates. It is with deep gratitude that I acknowledge their invaluable contributions.

To Michael Friedman and Karla Olson of the Friedman Group for seeing through an initial idea and supporting me during the critical early stages of development.

To Tim Frew, who patiently took my thoughts and edited them into a legible text.

To Mary Moriarty for continual support and trust in providing me the freedom with the rich variety of dried and preserved natural materials that added an essential dimension to the book.

To Barbara Miller of Hallmark Cards, Inc. for the candles and candlesticks that often accompany a garland and for the many gift wrapping and party paper products used throughout the book.

To John Riccardi and Rudy Grant of Seagroatt Floral Supply Company for the beautiful air-dried miniature roses and the spectacular fresh roses that I dried in silica gel. Seagroatt roses are the absolute best.

To Nancy Jones of Bob's Candy Co. that so amply kept the holiday spirit alive in midsummer with their candy canes, peppermints, and delightful peppermint rings.

To Robert Palmatier and Fredric Misner, who so generously provided a number of antiques from their Stone Ridge, N.Y. shop, as well as permitted me to harvest grapevines from their property and to borrow their freshly canned jellies and tomatoes.

To Aleene for her thick designer tacky glue which I find a great necessity when working with dried and preserved flowers.

To Donald Goncalves for providing me with Thermogrip® brand hot melt glue guns and glue sticks from Emhart Home Products Division. The ease and efficiency using a hot melt glue gun for constructing so many of the garlands was an essential tool and aid.

To Robert Hobermann whose sensitive eye and total understanding with the camera made the arduous task of photography a real pleasure. To Susan and Matthew for their patience and needed assistance.

To my wife Teri and son Jason who endured yet another inconvenience of having every available hook in our house occupied by a garland. To them and everyone else, my sincerest appreciation and thanks.

CONTENTS

Introduction

Once exclusively a symbol of the Christmas season and its spirit, garlands today are showing up in surprising places year-round. An herb garland in the kitchen, a doily garland in the bathroom or bedroom, a grapevine-and-dried-flower garland as a permanent decoration in the living room, a quilted garland in bright primary-colour fabric in the family room—all of these appear more often as people explore the fun and beautiful possibilities of the never-ending circle. In addition, new garlandmakers are surprised to find that with a little imagination and a few basic techniques garlandmaking can be a deceptively simple way to create decorations and gifts.

In recent years, there has been a growing appreciation of traditional handicrafts as well as a renewed interest in gardening, cooking, decorating, and just about anything having to do with rural life. As a result, the art of garlandmaking has progressed far beyond the habitual evergreen garland hanging on the door at Christmas. From simple country grapevine-and-herb garlands to elaborate garlands incorporating rare and exotic combinations of materials, this traditional rural handicraft has developed into an innovative and highly accessible art form.

Charming and imaginative garlands can be constructed using everything from dried flowers to children's building blocks. While garlandmaking is only limited by the imagination, some materials and techniques do lend themselves to garlandmaking better than others. This book of beautiful garlands is a treasure chest of ideas, techniques, and instruction. Some of the garlands covered here you may want to copy vine-for-vine, flower-for-flower, while others you may wish to alter in ways that will best suit your particular taste or specific needs. Within each chapter I have provided the essential steps for constructing individual garlands plus information on the kind of foundation used for each. There are also helpful tips on executing specific designs as well as general information on topics such as preserving flowers, tying foundations, attaching unusual ornaments, and more.

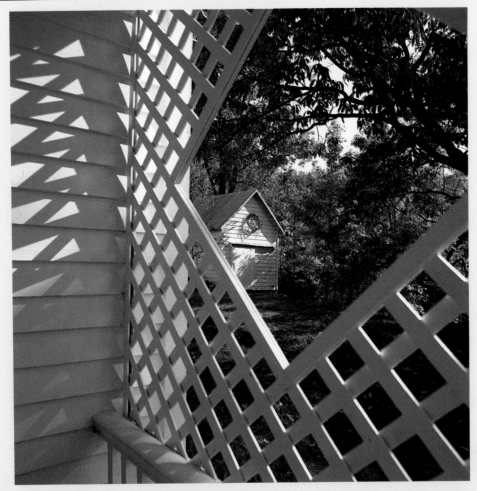

It is fair to say that some of the garlands illustrated here will be easier to duplicate than others. One reason is simply the availability of certain materials. However, one of the most enjoyable and challenging aspects of garlandmaking is the ability to make substitutions. You will find that any garland will gradually take on characteristics that reflect your own creativity. Once you have completed one garland, the door will remain open for continuing innovations and hours of enjoyment.

CHAPTER ONE

Getting Started

*G*arlandmaking can be a very rewarding experience, one that not only brings personal pride to the maker, but pleasure to all who see the results. Creating a garland, like all productive efforts, requires the proper tools and adequate space. This is not to say that you can't make the most spectacular arrangement of materials in conditions less than perfect, but the better your work area the easier it may be for a more fluid and productive execution of your talents.

Basically, you need two surfaces to work with. I prefer a wall when making most of my designs, but some garlands can only be developed on a table top. In my studio I have a solid nail in a wall that is directly perpendicular to my table. I can simply pivot myself from one surface to the other with great ease and directness. I have sufficient room to step back and see how a garland is developing on the wall, and yet be close enough to my worktable to have all the necessary tools and supplies at hand. I also have a large metal shelf unit at the far end of my worktable which houses boxes of supplies and dried materials.

A pegboard wall is a great place to store certain pieces of equipment and to hang garlands that are in the process of completion. Obviously, the degree of complexity or sophistication of a work space can be quite varied. It is possible to clean off the kitchen table and work with an equally successful outcome.

What seems basic and most essential is that you have a good area to work in with few obstacles to interrupt the construction process. The work area should be well lit with both natural and electrical light sources. If you rely only on electrical lights, try to prevent shadows on the work surface. Experiment by adding or moving lights until the work area is as bright and evenly lit as possible. I use clip-on lights with aluminium light shields, as they are flexible and inexpensive.

If you are creating a specific space to work in and will keep that space for continued garland-making, then consider the height of your worktable. In my studio I use a piece of plywood placed on top of two sawhorses. What I like about the sawhorses is that I can remove the top clamps or brackets and break down the legs for easy storage.

It is very important to have an electrical outlet near your work area. You will often use a hot-glue gun in garlandmaking, and there is no greater frustration than having to hunt down an outlet or precariously stretch a lead from a faraway socket to your work area. Good light, a proper and comfortable working height for your table, and a wall with a sturdy hook and an electrical outlet are the basics.

Complementing the basics is the proximity of adequate storage space. Grey industrial shelving is not only functional; it is also transportable. Easy to assemble and convenient to adjust, a wall of shelving can contain all the essentials you need from season to season. I gather and save all sorts of boxes, many in standardized proportions, that I fill and label and then stack on my shelves. Labelling them allows for stacking and not having to guess as seasons pass. I purchase boxes if I have to, but also go to local merchants and see what they are discarding.

Basic Tools

ONCE YOU HAVE CREATED A WORK SPACE, YOU WILL NEED the following tools to aid you in gathering materials and in constructing your garlands.

A good pair of basic garden clippers, capable of cutting through fairly substantial twigs and small branches, and a fairly sharp folding pocketknife are essential for gathering materials. Both the clippers and knife should be able to fit comfortably in a pocket as you take to the woods or fields in your gathering pursuits. I often find that a small saw is also helpful to have along. Some saws are small enough to be fixed within a sheath and attached to a belt, yet capable of cutting through a small tree or large branch. I find a light bow saw with a blade protector an easy component to any expedition. Depending on where you're going and what you're gathering purposes are, scissors might also be a sensible tool to have.

For your work area, you should have a pair of wire cutters, a pair of ribbon scissors, and a pair of garden shears to take care of your cutting needs. You will also quickly discover the value of a hot-glue gun as your garlandmaking interests expand. Hot-glue guns come in various sizes and price ranges. I have used a variety of them and prefer the larger ones with the trigger movement over the smaller ones, which operate by thumb pressure. What appeals to me is the freedom I have with the trigger gun, allowing better use of my hand and a greater ease in gluing. Both types work well, so research the various types to see which suits your garlandmaking needs.

A supply of craft wire (also called florist wire) is essential. This wire is handy for attaching pods or flowers to wooden picks, making a secure loop for hanging, or tying bows and other elements to the garland frame. You will also need wire to provide new stems for flowers that have been air-dried or silica-gel-dried.

While at the craft or florist shop, you will need to purchase wooden picks. These picks are either green or natural in colour, and come in a variety of lengths and widths. They have a thin wire on top for attaching the flower to the pick. Florist's picks are invaluable tools, so buy several of each size and keep them in a labelled storage box with other materials.

Florist tape works well for disguising wires and securing materials. I like the dark-green or dark-brown colours, because they blend with most of the materials I use. You'll find that with a little practice this tape is very easy to use. Simply start the end on a wire, then, with a gentle pull, spin the wire. The combination of pulling on the tape and spinning the wire will form a tight bond between the tape and the wire. A bottle or jar of white glue is also handy to have. You will find through experimentation and through conversation with other garlandmakers what product or tool is best to perform certain techniques. Take note, and add that tool to your basic materials.

Kenneth Spengler

Basic Tools Needed for Drying

YOU MIGHT WANT TO BEGIN PRESERVING YOUR OWN flowers. To do so, you will need to choose between air-drying them or preserving them in silica gel. For air-drying flowers and pods you will need some rubber bands and kitchen twine, brown paper bags, pushpins, cup hooks or nails, and either screening or a drying rack.

To dry flowers with silica gel you will need boxes of silica gel, available through craft and florist shops, and storage boxes. I also use masking tape to seal the lid of the box. Depending on which process you use, and on the durability of the flower, you will need additional boxes to store your preserved flowers. (See page 41 for more on preserving flowers with silica gel.)

Kenneth Spengler

Basic Garland Forms

WE WILL DEVOTE INDIVIDUAL CHAPTERS TO THE CONstruction of garland foundations as well as individual how-tos in making some of the illustrated garlands within this book, but you should be familiar with the kinds available to you through your local supply sources.

Grapevine garlands come in sizes that range from three-inch (eight-centimetre) garlands to very large, freshly wrapped garlands. The industry, both floral and craft, has produced grapevine garlands that not only come in natural colours but are also available in a palette of muted, vivid, or gilded colours. These coloured garlands spawn many decorative possibilities for your own creative expression. Wherever you find garlands sold, you will also see heart shapes made of grapevine. They too come in natural as well as tinted colours.

Another popular garland base that comes in a wide range of sizes is the straw garland. Basically, this is constructed of straw wound around a wire ring and secured with transparent nylon string. The straw garland base is tight and full, where similar artificial garlands have a softer and denser feeling to them. Artificial garlands are available in both circular and heart shapes, just like straw-based forms, but come in a range of decorative colours. Predominantly a craftstore item, these garlands seem to have gained popularity with craft classes.

Another versatile base is the Polystyrene base. Two versions are readily available. One is the simple form cut from foam, either green or white, and having flat sides. The second type of

foam garland is extruded foam. This type is usually reinforced with a wire ring and is capable of holding heavier weight.

The last type of base that is illustrated in this book is the wire ring. This, too, comes in a good range of sizes, as well as in heart shapes. They are versatile in making fresh garden garlands as well as garlands of permanent materials.

Kenneth Spengler

Things to Keep in Mind

IDEAS FOR GARLANDS COME FROM MANY SOURCES. Scanning through magazines, browsing through store displays, visiting other areas of the country—wherever you look you are bound to find materials and concepts that will spark your interests. As you come across garlands you would particularly like to copy, jot down a few notes on paper or try to sketch the general form. Ask about materials you do not recognize, and take advantage of walks through nature. Whether you're in the forest, at the seaside, or in your own backyard, you're sure to find something you can use for an attractive garland. If you plant a garden, then you are in for an endless harvest of possibilities.

Remember that you will be working with a circle, one of the most basic shapes. There are constraints placed upon this elementary shape, in that it begins and ends in a continuous line and often has a consistent width. It is best to approach garlandmaking with the understanding that, while the circle usually provides the base on which to apply and fix materials, it is your own individual treatment of the various foundations and materials that will allow you the greatest freedom.

Experiment and improvise; some of the most beautiful garlands have come from some of the most unusual combinations. You may choose to have long, trailing branches sweep the edge of your garland and flow toward the floor, while clusters of pods and flowers burst unexpectedly from areas around the circumference.

When designing garlands, scale is always an important consideration. Always keep in mind the intended resting place of the garland as you are making it. If you want to hang it on your front door, it must fit your front door. There is very little that is more frustrating than spending hours constructing a garland only to have it be too large or too small when it is finally finished. Avoid that frustration with careful planning and strategic execution. Your patience will reward you in the long run.

It is important to consider colour when developing your garland. In nature there is an incredible array of colours which can be combined to form garlands of absolute poetry. Strong, bold colours, vivid to the senses, powerful to the eye, are but one experience when working with colour. The subtle nuances that can come from combining delicate shades of one colour family or variations of soft pastels are counterparts to the fully saturated tones of the bolder palette. There are no limits to the combinations of colours you can use, nor are there limitations to the scale of flowers or their textures.

Perhaps the most interesting garlands are those that have an element of mystery and surprise to them. These unexpected qualities may easily come from a personalized interpretation of colours juxtaposed to one another, or to a surprising relationship in scale or texture. Visual richness, subtlety, and strength are all components to the overall texture of the garlandmaking process. To develop your skill in understanding more of this visual world, keep a watchful eye to the world as you walk in nature. Be aware of the unexpected and of the relationships of natural elements to each other. When you uncover a surprising quality about whatever it is you may be experiencing, try to translate that quality into your next garland.

Nature, of course, is the obvious teacher, but you can also learn many things from the library. Check out books not only on floral construction but on painting and art in general. See how other creative people bring their art to life by relating textures and colours.

Another good idea is to keep a few of the elements you are working with at hand. Place a pod or a few dried flowers near where you work, away from the area where you are constructing your garland, and occasionally look at the object, study it, and absorb it. Having a feeling for your materials will allow you the freedom to use unknown elements and still feel confident about your abilities. This confidence will let you experiment with colours that go beyond your personal preference, and soon you will be aware of your own growth as a creative person.

There are also some artistic elements to be aware of beyond colour and texture. Scale *must* be considered. Choosing shapes and objects that work well within the proportions of your garland will assure a visual balance. Establishing a rhythmic unity within the overall garland is vital to its appearance. That is to say that your garland should have a balance and counterbalance, each working to form a unified rhythmic

whole. The flowing parts of the garland should blend and become comfortable to the eye.

One of the most rewarding experiences of all in the process of garlandmaking is the gathering process. Growing flowers, harvesting them, and drying them involves the planting, the nurturing, and finally the rewards from picking and drying. I air-dry some and silica-gel-dry some and am always pleased when I discover other materials on walks and planned harvesting excursions. What you need in terms of materials has been covered: sharp scissors or a good pair of clippers, a pocketknife, and a good flat basket to carry your gathered flowers.

Here is a basic list of flowers and plants that work well in garlandmaking. This is for you to use as a reference, but by no means is this intended to limit your choices. Be willing to experiment with new materials all the time.

Garlandmaking Materials

ageratum	carnation	dock	gerbera	iris
ammobium	catmint	eucalyptus	germander	jasmine
anemone	celosia	fennel	globe amaranth	jonquil
aster	chamomile	fern	goldenrod...in bud	lady's-mantle
astilbe	cockscomb	feverfew	heliotrope	lamb's ears
baby's breath	cornflower	flax	hibiscus	larkspur
bellflower	daffodil	forget-me-not	hollyhock	lavender
black-eyed Susan	dahlia	foxglove	honeysuckle	lemon balm
borage	daisy	freesia	hydrangea	lemon leaves
box calendula	delphinium	geranium	hyssop	lilac

Anita Marci

Anita Marci

Mary Close

Mary Close

Mary Close

Anita Marci

lily	peony	sea holly	tulip
lily-of-the-valley	petunia	silver king	Veronica
loosestrife	pink	southernwood	violet
marigold	pussy willow	statice	wild grass
monkshood	ranunculus	stock	wormwood
mint	rose	strawflower	yarrow
mugwort	rose leaf	sunflower	zinnia
nasturtium	rosemary	tansy	
orange blossom	rue	teasel	
Queen Anne's lace	sage	thistle	
pansy	salvia	thyme	

CHAPTER TWO
Grapevine Garlands

*T*o me, there is nothing more satisfying than to travel the countryside in search of grapevines. With garden clippers and a thermos of hot coffee in hand, the hunt becomes one of autumn's greatest adventures. It is best to harvest grapevines in the autumn, when they are brown and the leaves are turning golden. Early-summer vines are too green and will crack at the simplest bend, causing unnecessary frustration.

If you choose not to weave your own grapevine garlands, you can buy them at most flower, garden, and craft shops. Popular as well as plentiful, they are available in a number of sizes and surface treatments—including the ever-popular vine heart, a number of which are illustrated throughout this book.

*O*n a loosely woven, handmade vine garland, I have randomly applied preserved autumn leaves with a hot-glue gun. The colours of the leaves vary from rust to a bright yellow. I have intertwined them with the garland in such a way that they stick out prominently in some places but are tucked within the ribs of the vines in others. This gives the garland its natural, spontaneous look. Three sea-grape leaves form a focal point at the top of the composition. Garden strawflowers provide colour and scale contrast to the natural pinecones that cluster around the garland. Lovely lavender statice travels throughout the warmer strawflower's colours, tying all the neutral elements together, while the lunaria add lustre to the overall composition with patches of lightness.

This harvest garland uses materials that are easily available through local garden shops, craft stores, and florists; growing your own strawflowers, statice, and lunaria makes for an even more satisfying garland at harvest time. Adding materials such as sea-grape leaves brings an unexpected element of surprise to the garland.

25

How to Make a Grapevine Base

THE PROCESS OF MAKING A GRAPEVINE WREATH IS RE-ally a very simple one that becomes even more so with practice. Hold the cut end of a vine in your left hand, and with your right hand bend the free end of the vine into a circle, approximating the desired proportion of the final garland. Clasp that section of the vine with your left hand. Your hand now holds the loop that will become the vine base. With your right hand weave the free end of the vine in and out, through the loop, securing the two ends by locking them into the vine.

Start your second length of vine by inserting one end into the woven part of the first loop. Weave the length of the second vine through the base and secure the ends. With each length of vine your garland will grow in width. Continue this process until you achieve the desired fullness. When ending the garland, tuck all the loose ends into the body of the base.

Another method of making a vine garland is to start with three vines, and, while holding them in your left hand, twist them together so that they form a rope-like singular vine. When adding additional vines, continue to twist each one around so that the final, full garland is even and dense. Again, tuck all loose ends into the body of the garland after you've reached the desired width.

I always prefer to make my garlands very full and somewhat irregular instead of even and pristine. The reasoning is that the garland will be able to hold more objects in unexpected places if it is strong and full—allowing more freedom in the design.

After wrapping my garlands I always add a wire loop to the top for hanging. This gives me a reference point for the top of the garland as well as a safeguard for holding the vines together. Be sure the wire loop is strong and securely attached. Many hours of fine work can be lost in an instant if your creation falls off the hook because of a loose wire. It you finish your garland and realize you forgot to add a hanging wire, be very careful not to harm your work when threading the wire through the vine. An extra pair of hands can be very welcome.

Although wrapping a grapevine garland is relatively easy, it is very important to pay attention to how tight you wrap the vines as you go along. The degree of firmness or looseness of the vine will strongly influence the final look of the garland. Experimentation is the key here. The more garlands you make, the greater control you will have. No matter what size garland you are attempting, the process is the same; always remember to lock the starting vines together and weave in the remaining vines. If you finish a vine base that satisfies your needs, but still have extra vines, take the time to wind another, perhaps smaller one. The excitement of making a garland is such that when you have completed one you'll most likely want to begin another. Remember, too, that a small garland is always a great gift to have on hand; so make extras to "save for a rainy day."

In method one, wrap one length of vine at a time, weaving new lengths around the main body of the wreath until reaching the desired width.

In method two, start with three vines and twist them together so they form a ropelike singular vine. Add more vines to reach the desired width.

Kenneth Spengler

hile exploring the forest floor or open fields in the autumn, or while taking a holiday to another part of the country, you are bound to come across some unusual pods or other dried materials. Such discoveries can be exciting and can lead to wonderful collections. While these natural treasures make some of the most rewarding materials, many very exotic flowers, pods, and plants are available through your local florist and craft stores and can add much to your overall design. These materials are collected from all over the world and made ready for your creative use.

In this example, I have wrapped some lengths of bleached vines around a natural vine garland and have then added clusters of sea-grape leaves as well as an array of bleached and preserved pods. Chico, chokeberry, curly protea, flat canella, and sponge mushrooms all add their independent shapes and textures in bringing a harmonic blend of browns and beiges to this garland. If you can't find the specific pod you want, substitute nuts, pinecones, bits of bark, or even cork to carry on the monochrome palette of this design.

*I*n order to achieve the delicate lacy feeling of this garland, I covered a pre-made vine heart base with sprigs of fresh silver king. Pieces of thin florist's wire works well for attaching the fragile silver king into place. The preserved yellow flowers add a warm contrast to the soft grey of the silver king. The addition of fresh bayberry and bud clusters from flat-leaf eucalyptus complement the overall grey colouration, while keeping their own independence. To bring out the pale green of the eucalyptus, I added a soft moss-green ribbon with a subtle edge of gold. Lavender statice provides a colour complement to the yellow flowers. I used a hot-glue gun to attach all the components together. Again, always remember to first attach a hanging hook to your frame before adding any elements to the garland.

*M*any garlands are meant to last—to echo the season and reflect the beauty of nature for as long as the materials hold up. Some garlands, however, are spontaneous expressions of a particular moment in time.

In this autumn celebration, baby pumpkins, gourds, bittersweet, strawflowers, and sunflowers unite with the bold vibrancy of cockscombs, Japanese lanterns, and vivid purple statice; the expression becomes a magnificent salute to the brilliant energies of autumn. This composition was placed upon a richly dyed burgundy grapevine garland in order to help bring out the intense colours and bold shifts in scale of each element. Many pre-made vine garlands come in a spectacular array of colours—boldly saturated as well as pastel. Vine colours can be used to enhance or complement the added materials—as in this example. When you make a garland such as this, understand that it may go through some natural changes, so be ready to continue adding other durable elements as some of the more perishable ones depart. A garland can become an ongoing adventure.

Here, the bittersweet seems to explode from the regimented contour of the garland form, much as it does when growing in the wild. Other elements, such as the gourds and the Japanese lanterns, are clustered in groups. The whole composition nearly fills the substructure, but leaves just enough visible base to enjoy the unexpected coloured vine. Although this garland is hung, consider laying it flat as a centrepiece on a holiday table.

The personality of the vine garland itself is sometimes the element that first speaks to the viewer. There are a number of choices when making them. In this one I used rather thick vines to determine the finished form. I intentionally left great holes within the structure of the garland while enhancing the natural beauty of the grapevine with the inclusion of fresh clusters of grapes and grape leaves. As the grapes and the leaves dried they became very brittle but still retained their leafy identity. While sometimes I feel that a smooth, uniform garland is more suitable for a specific design, here I preferred to allow much of the nature of the grapevine to come forth. The deep and open segments in the vine construction are natural places to cluster cockscomb, yarrow, and stems of flat-leaf eucalyptus. Small branches of fresh bayberry bring a lighter tonal value to the deeper, more intense colours of the yarrow and cockscomb. The contrast helps the eye to travel around the composition.

How to Air-dry Flowers

MOST OF THE FLOWERS USED IN THE PREVIOUS GARLAND are air-dried—a simple process anyone can do without much trouble. To air-dry flowers from your garden, simply pick the individual flowers during the drier part of the day, when the dew has evaporated and the sun has begun to warm the earth. Strip their leaves and tie them into small bunches of three to five stems. Hang the stems up in a dry, dimly lit part of the house, such as an attic or a closet. Try to avoid dusty places. If that isn't possible, then place your flowers in a large paper bag, tying the top of the bag to the flower stems. Invert the bag and hang to dry. Drying time will depend on the amount

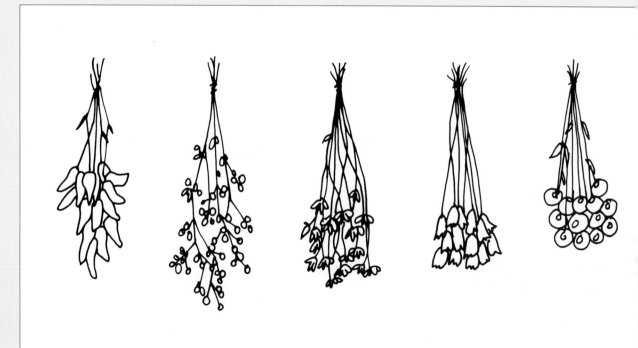

of air, heat, and moisture in the room. Check the flowers from day to day and remove them when the flower petals feel like paper and are no longer soft and pliable. When storing the dried flowers, keep them away from excessive moisture and direct sunlight. Both conditions will shorten the life of the flower.

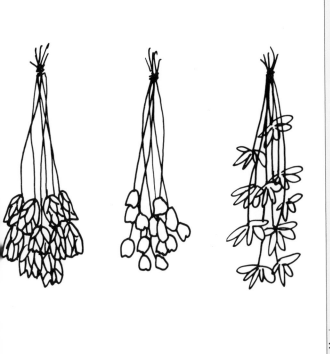

Anita Marci

Kenneth Spengler

Another method for air-drying flowers is to lay them on a screen in the attic or under a bed. Newspaper also works, as long as you remember the necessary ingredients—low light and warm, dry air. Experimentation is essential in determining what works best for your particular situation.

*T*his hydrangea garland is another example of a garland that celebrates a specific moment in the evolution of autumn. It consists of only hydrangeas, a flower made up of many smaller flowers. Although they have different tonalities and sizes, their appearance expresses a general unity. There is a soft fullness to the flower, and delicate shadings of colour. Using a variety of blossom sizes and weaving them into a very aggressive vine garland brings two juxtaposed elements into a unified whole. Allowing the vine to dominate the positioning of the flowers, I hot-glued the hydrangeas throughout the large-scaled garland. The uniformity of the flowers and subtle blending of the colouration keeps the scale of the garland under control.

  This pre-made heart with silica-gel dried wild roses is akin to the hydrangea garland in that both use a single flower and expose some of the vine structure. While the great swells of the hydrangea bring that garland its softness, the rose heart relies on the relationship of the sparse, delicate rose to the heart shape. Rose clusters are placed along the sides of the heart, while vertically placed roses join together in the junction at the top. The leaves enhance the heart shape, fill in the width, and support the sprigs of rose clusters. I took special care to match the scale of the heart to the scale of the flowers—as I did for the hydrangea garland above. Scale is an important factor in establishing a visual presence to the garland. If the elements are too large, it may become overpowering; if they're too small or sparse, it may lack interest. Balance, scale, rhythm, and colour relationships are major considerations when making a garland. (See Chapter One, "Getting Started," for more discussion of these topics.)

*T*his strawflower garland is another example of the use of a pre-made vine heart. Here, I harvested my own strawflowers and then inserted florist wire into the heads of each flower and hung them to dry.

When they were ready, I first attached the lighter strawflowers with a hot-glue gun around the heart in a way that evenly distributed the colour variations. Next I brought in a darker flower tone, and after that the deepest colours. Finally, I included the white sprigs of stringia, which added a lightness in scale and colour to the overall warm, dense composition.

Fill an airtight container about two-thirds full with silica gel, gently place the flowers on top, and then gently sprinkle more gel on top until the flowers are completely covered. Seal the container for about three or four days. When the flowers are completely dry, carefully remove them with a slotted spoon.

Drying Flowers with Silica Gel

IT IS A GREAT FEELING TO GO INTO YOUR GARDEN AND PICK flowers or herbs that you've grown, bring them back to your house, and use them, either directly in cooking, in a fresh arrangement, or drying them for use at a later time. It is also sad when seasons change and you no longer have the special flowers of spring or early summer to use or appreciate. Silica gel allows you the privilege of saving what is usually transitory.

Silica gel is a sand-like substance that dries flowers within a few days. It can be purchased at most craft stores and is very convenient to use. All you need is a box of gel and a few airtight container such as plastic storage boxes. The process of drying must be done in airtight containers to prevent outside moisture from reaching the flowers. The silica gel removes moisture from the flowers, making them usable for garlands as well as dried arrangements and potpourri.

Here are a few basic steps in drying flowers with silica gel. Fill an airtight container about two-thirds full with the gel. Lay each flower in the gel, petals up. Very gently sprinkle the remaining gel around and over each flower, being careful to fill in between the petals, until the flowers are completely covered. Seal the container and in three days check the progress. In most cases I have found that three or four days does the trick, but heavy-stemmed, thick-petaled flowers may require more time.

Removing the dried flowers is perhaps the trickiest part of the process, because they have now become very fragile and can easily break apart. The best method is to place a slotted spoon under the petals and gently lift the flower out. After removing the flowers, store them in another plastic box with a quarter inch (four millimetres) of gel covering the bottom.

This process allows you to keep out-of-season flowers for use later on, providing a floral vocabulary that extends the range and variety of flowers year-round. The silica-gel process works not only with homegrown flowers but with store-bought flowers as well. The key element to remember is that the flowers should be dry and fresh when placed in the gel. The fresher the flower, the more successful the result. This is also a trial-and-error process, so don't become discouraged if the petals fall off your first batch. Glue works wonders and can be used to replace missing petals.

Kenneth Spengler

Use a paint brush and a small bit of glue to replace any petals that may have fallen off.

*T*his small, handmade vine garland is ornamented with silica-gel-dried black-eyed Susans, a few acorns, and preserved leaves. Many of the twigs from the original grapevine are still attached. The inherent rhythm of this garland comes from the juxtaposition of the twigs and the variation in scale of the dried flowers. It is made up of individual clusters of flowers, with equal space allotted for the vine itself. With this garland it is important to show as much of the garland form as possible in order to take advantage of the unique, personal quality of the attached twigs.

43

*T*raditionally, garlands have been used as decorative accents at time of celebration. The festive presence of this wedding garland almost seems to ring in an abundant sound of joy through the many paper bells attached to the pre-made, white-painted vine garland. Silver ribbon and silver stars accent the fullness of the wedding bells, and add to the festiveness of the garland. It should be mentioned that all garlands need not be made of flowers and that a garland of wrapped packages makes a wonderful holiday or birthday centrepiece, each child or adult receiving a gift as the packages are taken from the garland. Holiday bells in red and green are a perfect accompaniment to evergreens or a painted vine base. The fact is that there are many unusual materials that can make delightful and unique garlands. Visit card stores, craft shops, and floral shops, and keep abreast of new ideas.

A variation on this garland is to add fresh flowers by inserting them into water picks, available at your local florist, and placing them amidst the bells. Your garland can become as complex as you wish, as long as you keep the design proportionate to the base. This wedding-bell garland can be taken apart, as the bells collapse and are simply tied on. This allows you the opportunity to create another festive wedding garland when the next bride calls.

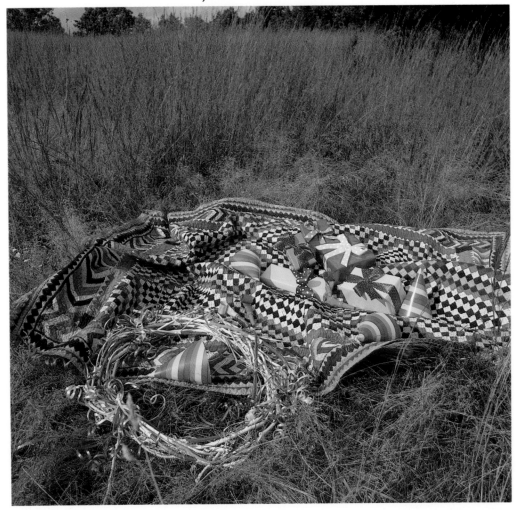

*T*his garland offers some unusual yet simple ideas for a colourful party decoration. Spray-paint a vine garland a solid colour, then hand-paint some stripes that correspond to gift wrapping paper and add yards of curling ribbon. Wrap packages for each child in the colours of the garland, then take the whole party out into the fields, your garden, or someplace where fun has no boundaries. The scale and colours of this party garland can be altered to fit a number of situations and environments.

45

resh flowers attached to a garland do very well for a limited period of time if they are first placed in water tubes. As mentioned before, water tubes are available through your florist in a number of shapes and sizes. Add a few fresh flowers, perhaps a bright ribbon, and hang this beautiful and seasonal presentation on your door. It will reflect your creativity as well as the completeness of your party preparations.

A variation on this garland would be to add some small succulents or some ivy. In all the examples within this book there are many variations and substitutions that can be made. If you don't have a particular ingredient for one of these garlands, improvise. You will be surprised at how varied a garland can be.

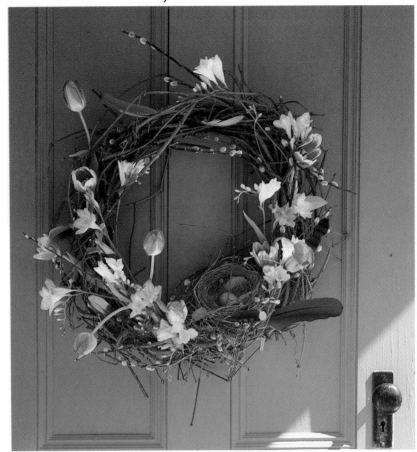

*S*pring flowers, again in water tubes; an abandoned bird's nest; a few feathers—each of these elements were added for their particular form and colour. When the pussy willows appear and winter still has a leg in the door, cheer up your house or table with a spring garland. It may only last a few days, but it will bridge the changing of the seasons. Create a fresh-flower garland for a special party or meeting, or as a "thinking-of-you" gift. By refilling the water picks you can lengthen the life of the fresh flowers and thus prolong the beauty of the garland. You may want to design the garland so that when you remove the flowers, and their water tubes, you have the bird's nest and a few colourful feathers left to enjoy. If you are making this garland for Easter, try blowing out some eggs, dyeing or painting them bright colours, and hot-gluing them among the flowers, thus making this garland both fuller and more festive.

lthough this particular heart is pre-made, it is a simple process to make your own. First make a beginning, heart-shaped form out of wire—a coat hanger will do. Then place the cut grapevines onto the heart shape and, with thin florist wire, wire them in place. It is possible to attach three or four vines at once to create a fuller form. Always remember to use a thin-gauge florist wire to secure the vines. You will want to cover the construction with flowers when finished. Also remember to always place a hanging hook at the top of every garland before adding any ornaments. A finished garland can be very cumbersome to handle.

This heart has a combination of commercially dried black-eyed Susans, as well as a few pansies, some lichen, and pieces of sheet moss. A few sprigs of berries and a satin ribbon add to the ingredients. The combined use of silica-gel flowers and available dried flowers provides a personalized touch. The use of the unexpected adds great charm and alters the look of your creation.

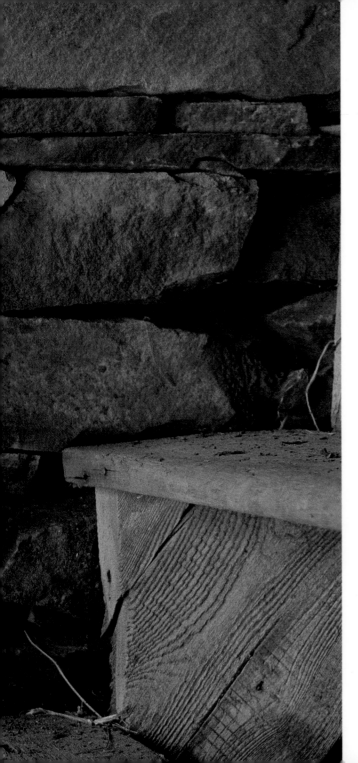

A commercially bleached garland with pods, yellow roses, and cornhusks makes this tailored garland appear very snug. Clusters of cornhusk loops form a generous bow at the top of the garland. This cluster mirrors a similar cluster of yellow roses and pods. The cornhusk loops were wired onto short florist picks and directly inserted into the garland structure. A touch of glue from a hot-glue gun holds each pick in place. The dried roses, ferns, and pods were also glued fast to prevent them from falling off. A tailored garland of such paleness and symmetry can be used in a number of settings throughout the home for a variety of occasions.

Whereas the previous garland feels hard and very controlled, this sumptuous heart evokes a purely romantic feeling. It employs a great variety of summer flowers, mixing together colours and textures as well as scales. Using silica-gel dried flowers hot-glued onto a pre-made heart base, this heart includes the richest examples of the early-summer garden and the late-spring bounty. Peonies, summer roses, wild sunflowers, Queen Anne's lace, and black-eyed Susans from the fields combine with sprigs of wild roses and bachelor's buttons. Shades of orange and pink, deep rich reds, and vibrant blues nest together with a few wild leaves. The heart has symmetry and fullness while evoking lovely surface grace and beauty.

*I*n early autumn I often make a large vine garland and begin collecting fallen bird's nests, a wasp's nest or two, and dried sunflowers. I gather them together to make an ongoing garland. They become gatherings, each version an addition or subtraction to the last, and always dependent on the wonders that are found in nature. A branch or two of brilliant-coloured leaves enhances the kaleidoscope of colours that grace the gathering garland. When the snows cover the land, I like to add berries of cedar and juniper to the vine, along with winter redberries and evergreen boughs. I like to keep the bold bare garland for the rest of the year and hang it on the outside of a building—both to fill the space and to recall the garland's earlier styles.

CHAPTER THREE

Wire Garlands

T here are endless possibilities for creating beautiful and imaginative gar-lands—the chapter on grapevines only tapped the surface. The basic truth about garlandmaking as a handicraft is that the possibilities are endless. Your explorations can be as varied as flowers are available. By changing one flower or a combination of flowers in one design, you can come up with what looks like an entirely different garland.

Wire rings are a very useful base on which to construct a garland. They are available in a number of sizes and weights to support various sizes and weights of ornaments. Be careful when selecting the ring: Make sure that it will suit your requirements. As in preparing to make a wire garland—and with *all* garlands—remember to attach a hanging loop.

For this lovely heart garland I wired sprigs of fresh rosemary, sage, and mint to the base and then used a hot-glue gun to attach strips of cinnamon to the herbs. At the top of the heart, delicate silica-gel-dried roses were glued into place along with a few small pinecones. The deep brown of the pinecones complements the soft golden colour of the rose.

This garland is secure, because the wire holding the fresh herbs has a firm grip on the wire base and the hot-glue does a tremendous job of anchoring the light elements.

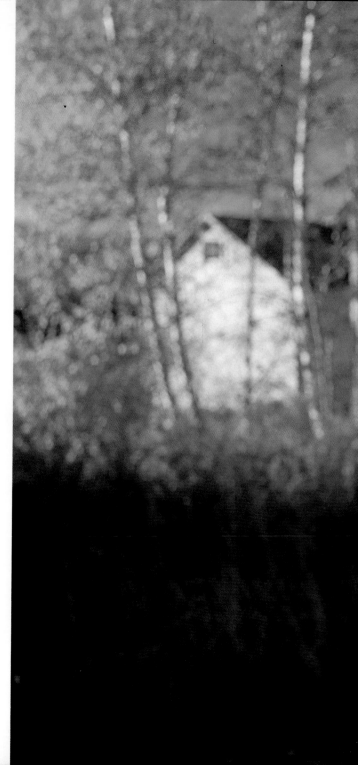

*A*nother small garland constructed from a wire base is
this moss-covered one with
pink roses and dusty miller.
Apply hot glue to the sheet moss and carefully fold it
around and over the wire frame, squeezing it to form a
snug covering. Add more moss if necessary, until you
achieve the desired fullness. When the moss is secure,
attach clusters of rose hips, individual leaves from a
dusty miller plant, and some beautifully opened silica-
gel-dried roses with a hot-glue gun. Rose hips can be
found in the wild during autumn, or they can be bought
from your florist along with the roses. Allow the roses to
open before you dry them, but keep in mind that for
best results it is important to dry flowers when they are
fresh. Pop the roses into the gel as soon as they reach the
degree of openness you desire.

   To dry dusty miller, either dry individual leaves on a
screen or pop them into the silica gel, too. I find air-
drying whole plants to be interesting.

ire rings are wonderful to use after harvesting a group of flowers and herbs from the garden. The entire picking process is heightened by the expectation of turning the fruits of your garden into a beautiful dried garland that will last for a year or more. A great deal of satisfaction can be gained from growing, harvesting, and drying virtually all of your garland materials. This garland is entirely made of materials grown in my garden.

62

Winding a Garland

TO WIND A WREATH ON A WIRE FRAME YOU FIRST NEED TO clear off a good working surface (see Chapter One—Getting Started). A kitchen table is fine, as is a workbench or picnic table. If your knees are good and your back isn't stiff, the ground works equally well. You will need a pair of garden snippers, a spool of waxed twine (waxed twine grips the flower stems better than unwaxed), and, of course, a wire ring with a loop at the top.

Begin to make a general selection of what flowers you have and what additional material you expect to put into your garland. The only hitch in winding a garland is that once you begin it is not possible to stop and add additional elements, so be sure to plan ahead.

After deciding what elements you will be using, take a few of the flowers and place them on the wire frame. Hold the frame and the flowers in your left hand and place a length of twine alongside the flower stems. With your right hand, wind the spool of twine through and around the base in a clockwise direction and secure the twine so that it doesn't unravel. Be sure to wind a few turns around the garland with each cluster of flowers, making sure all elements are tight and secure. This process of winding in a clockwise direction in a continual spiral motion is the manner in which the entire garland will be wound. Each time you have secured a handful of flowers to the frame, reapply another cluster of flowers or herbs. An important note: include small bunches of flowers so that they cover the outer and inner edges of the garland.

When you are nearly at the end of the garland and are approaching the starting point, be extra careful that you don't bruise the lead flowers. Gently lift their heads up and place the stems of the tail-end flowers into place, wind with care, and finally secure the twine with a few good knots. If the construction has a noticeable gap, I sometimes take a few flowers, wire them to a short florist pick, and insert the pick into the open area.

Don't worry about using too many flowers in a winding garland; a fuller garland seems to look better than one where the mechanics are exposed. This winding process allows you to make a number of garland combinations using a great variety of materials, as well as a number of ring sizes. The more practice you have, the easier this process will become.

Kenneth Spengler

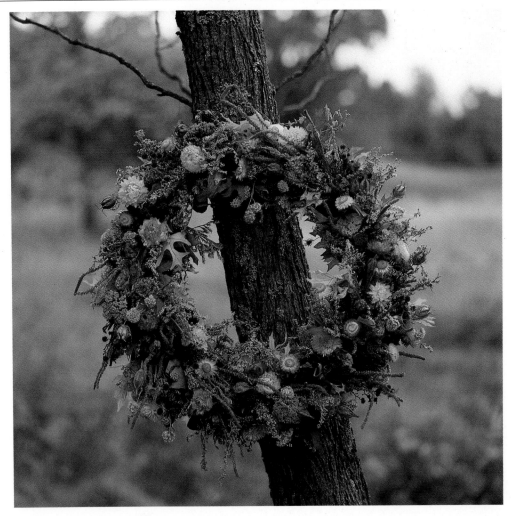

The following two examples are really variations on the autumn combinations seen in the previous garland. Each one has used a selection of strawflowers, sage, rosemary, German statice (which is white), coloured statice, silver king, yarrow, nigella, dried roses, and a pod or two.

Variations on the fullness and overall texture are up to you. To make multiple garlands of a particular style, simply note the general amount of materials needed and reserve an equal portion for the next garland.

*J*ust like the grapevine garlands, wire frames are available in both ring and heart forms. This chili heart was made by opening one end of the heart frame and stringing on enough chilis to form a compact line of peppers. The ends at the lower point of the heart frame are joined together by two loops. This makes a great garland that complements the decor of any kitchen, and is a wonderful gift for someone who is fond of cooking.

66

*P*aper ribbon is a popular item available at craft stores and florist shops. Here, I covered a small wire ring with paper ribbon, culminating with a big paper bow on the top. Next, I strung small red peppers on a sturdy thread and wound them around the covered frame, securing both ends behind the bow. I then wired garlic and a few sprigs of sage onto the knot of the bow. This little garland is right at home in the kitchen, where the cook can systematically remove the ingredients throughout the winter and then refill the garland come late summer.

This harvest garland of strawberry popcorn and silver king was made by using waxed twine and a medium-sized wire frame. To wind this garland, I began with the centre ear, adding a few pieces of silver king and ears to cover the inner and outer edges. Because the popcorn ears are heavy, it is very important to wind a few extra turns of the twine so that the garland remains very tight. The silver king softens the overall dominance of the cornhusks, and breaks up the beige that would otherwise overpower the garland.

The last illustration of a wire garland is this full rose-hip garland, which uses the same winding construction as the previous few garlands. Simply gather the rose-hip clusters in small bunches and wind the twine to secure. A real warning: Rose hips are very difficult to harvest; their sharp thorns can prick your arms and hands.

CHAPTER FOUR

Straw-based Garlands

The straw base is perhaps the most versatile of all garland bases. It consists of tightly packed rings of straw bound together by a transparent thread. Coming in a number of sizes, the girth of straw garlands makes them especially suitable for inserting picked material. You can purchase these in nearly all florist shops, craft stores, and even some fabric centres.

*T*his garland of wheat, rye, and wild oats was made by taking three or four pieces of each element, one by one, and wiring them onto a three-inch (8–centimetre) wooden pick. I then followed a clockwise direction, inserting each element into the straw until the whole base was covered by a gentle blending of the three different materials. This blending creates a change in the texture of the garland and an interplay with light that shifts the tonalities of the overall complexion of the garland. The result is a monochrome garland that is still very complex in its texture and surface. Try different variations of this garland by substituting different grasses from the fields or by using only one material and varying its length and texture.

F or this harvest garland I twisted long lengths of raffia together and wrapped them onto the lower portion of a straw ring. I then added corn and chili peppers to the top of the garland. The small ears of corn were attached by wiring them onto florist picks and inserting them into the base. The corn became a cascade, as one ear overlapped another, forming a great tuft of husks at the top. The small hot peppers were strung on a durable string and tied around the central stack of husks. By allowing the raffia to remain a little free, I feel I created a more interesting texture.

77

his autumn-leaf garland is yet another example of using florist's picks to attach materials to the base. Using oak leaves that were treated to remain flexible, I chose colours that flowed from yellow to orange to rust and attached them in a process very similar to the wheat construction (page 75). Broad colour areas direct the eye around the garland and aid in creating the sweeping movement of colour within the structure.

I

t seemed essential to include a straw heart, as we have used heart frames within each chapter. Here I have combined the straw heart with one of the most traditional garland forms—the pinecone garland. There are many ways to make a pinecone garland, the most common one being to wire each pinecone and to individually attach them according to size around a double wire frame. Many wonderful patterns develop from the varying sizes and textures of pinecones.

This pinecone heart is a departure from the very exacting methods of wire-frame construction. A straw-heart base is the support for pre-picked pinecone rosettes. The picks are already inserted into the crown of the cone, making the process of creating the symmetrical heart relatively simple. First, sort out the rosettes according to size. Starting with the smaller cones, begin attaching the rosettes in such a way that they form patterns of textural interest.

*T*his moss-and-lichen garland is another very simple one to construct. Using sheet moss to cover the straw base, I added pieces of wood moss, reindeer moss, and giant reindeer moss, each available through florist shops, as well as lichen that I picked up on a walk through the woods. The fullness of this garland is an exercise in placement. The hot-glue gun easily set down the general distribution of the colours and variety of textures provided by the moss. The challenge is to create interesting clusters for the eye so that the general texture of the garland is not monotonous. The characteristics of each moss made it possible to attach each clump to another at angles that enhance the overall rhythm of the garland surface. Bits of leaves and pine needles have been left in the lichen to extend the natural charm of this type of garland.

ere, I covered a very small heart of straw with a coat of sheet moss, glued down with a hot-glue gun. A cluster of pansies and Johnny-jump-ups, all dried in silica gel, ornaments the surface. The size variations and colour changes keep the surface of this heart interesting. It is a perfect little garland for a gift—delicate and special through the combinations of moss and flowers, as well as its general scale.

*T*his summer garland consists of preserved ferns covering a straw base. The vivid green fern brings out the deep magenta of the cockscomb, the pale contrast of the bleached grapevine, the burgundy-to-gold shading of the strawflowers, and the soft lavender statice. There are a number of treated ferns available through your florist. Each will bring a grace and softness to a garland while adding the summer spirit to other flowers.

In this example, small clusters of the fern were wired to florist's picks and inserted into the straw base. When the garland was full, I took longer lengths of the fern and picked them among the shorter clusters, which extended the flowing softness of the surface. It is important to allow the edge of the garland a little freedom of movement. Once the fern was placed, I wired the ends of the bleached grapevine onto picks, anchored one end to the base, and weaved the vine through the centre into a pleasing rhythm before securing the other end to the frame. Finally, I added a few sprigs of baby's breath to lighten the whole garland and add a lovely summer touch. Each flower was either picked or placed with the help of the hot-glue gun.

*T*he broadness of the straw base allows for real expansion when winding a garland (see page 63 for information on winding a garland). This example has been made by winding using waxed twine, though some elements have been picked into the finished garland. This is truly an autumn symphony of all flowers, both air-dried as well as purchased, including fresh herbs and lengths of cinnamon. To duplicate this garland, you could combine garden flowers, store-bought flowers, and any unexpected wild things you might find. One of the greatest delights in garlandmaking is that you can use virtually any material as long as you are pleased with the general tonalities of the entire composition.

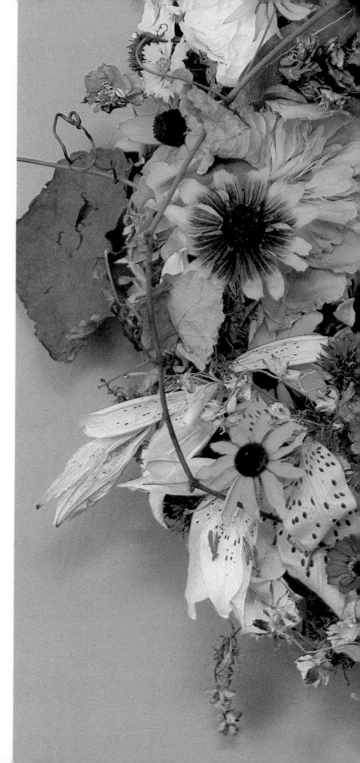

There is a great deal of activity going on with this silica-gel-dried garland. Flowers peek out from underneath others; colours brush against colours; petals intermingle with leaves. Pink peonies, pale-yellow tiger lilies, bright-hued zinnias, and delicate delphinium contrast against the more vivid deep orange and yellow of summer daisies, black-eyed Susans, and bachelor buttons. Among the varieties of flowers I used are wild roses and marigolds; bits of pale lichen and deeper-coloured sheet moss assist in filling in some of the visual pockets. Each flower was dried in silica gel, a process that took many weeks and may easily be the final statement of a season's labour. The garland is tightly constructed, yet the random leaves fall into an irregular pattern, allowing the eye to move about in a less regimented way. Keep an unexpected spirit to your creations and they will remain interesting to you and to others for a long period of time.

*T*his picked pod garland creates a bold impression with its tones of whitewashed grey. There is a boldness and directness to each element, and from the beginning to the end each pod holds its own space with its own distinctive shape. Although these whitewashed pods are available from your local florist, it is also possible to do the job yourself. All you need are a few old rags, a bucket of white paint, and a two-inch (five·centimetre) brush to penetrate all the deep crevices in the pods. I suggest using water-soluble acrylic paint to keep the cleaning-up process as simple as possible.

Simply dip each pod into the bucket of paint until the paint saturates the pod. Remove the pod from the bucket and let the excess drip off. Then gently wipe off more paint until there is a thin, even coat of paint on the pod.

When you place the pods into the straw base, fill in the garland with individual pods, then add some sprigs of German statice to soften the overall line of the garland. The statice is similar in colour to the pods, but has a softness that provides a textural contrast to the more rigid pods, lending a balance to the overall effect.

*O*ne of the great joys of garlandmaking is that it can be done just for the fun of it. A remembrance of a summer holiday by the sea can become the foundation for a beautiful summer garland. Here, Spanish moss was hot-glued to the straw frame to form the base for the decorative shells. I attached the shells to florist picks with a hot-glue gun and then inserted them into the base at angles, in order to keep the surface alive with an independent energy. Black-eyed Susans and lovely blue larkspur flowers were glued among the shells and pieces of coral. The finishing touch to this garland came with a thin satin bow with trailing streamers. The ribbon added an element of grace to the garland.

Remember to alter the scale of the shells you use so that the garland doesn't feel too regulated, and keep the shells at soft angles to one another. This, too, keeps the surface more alive. What appears in nature is an ever-changing cycle, an ever-moving line. A garland should seem almost alive as it hangs on your wall or graces your table.

A very similar foundation to straw is Polystyrene, in that it comes in about the same sizes and dimensions. There are some advantages to working with Polystyrene, one being that the stems of flowers penetrate it rather easily. It is lightweight and holds most materials very well. My principle objection to Polystyrene is that it has a tendency to split when you use heavy materials, so it must be reinforced. However, I do find it a very suitable base for the garlands illustrated here.

*T*his harvest garland was constructed using a repetitive spiral placement, employing a variety of materials, each represented by an individual colour and texture. Pink larkspur, grey silver king, deep berry, and pale-green sage are the dominating arms of this wheel, while nigella, yarrow, and purple statice add their complementary textures.

Each stem was inserted directly into the Polystyrene. It is important to make sure to cover the inside and outside edges of the garland and to cut the stems according to your specific needs.

The same construction techniques were used in making this eucalyptus garland: Short lengths of the stems were cut and directly inserted into the foam base. Longer lengths were then added to give the garland fullness as well as grace. Once again, the stem lengths were cut at varying lengths to avoid the possibility that the final garland would look as if a computer made it. Life for a garland comes through the play of one element against another.

I enjoy making garlands using basically only one type of material. Again, this silver-king garland was constructed the same way as the eucalyptus garland on the previous page.

My only words of advice in making a garland of this type are to keep it free, open, and loose. Let the sunlight play off the surface and watch the beautiful inner shadows develop throughout the day and in the changing season. This garland, like the eucalyptus garland, can be hung almost anywhere and makes a perfect gift.

To construct this child's wreath, fill the whole surface, including both inner and outer edges, with small bunches of prepared baby's breath attached to small wooden picks. Then attach the baby blocks on a proportionately smaller wire ring. Hot-glue the blocks with three lengths of florist's picks and, when dry, insert them into the foam base at angles to the surface of the wreath. The little trucks, boats, and cars could be exchanged for little dolls or animals. Add a ribbon to the top of the composition and you have a great wreath to hang in a child's or grandchild's room.

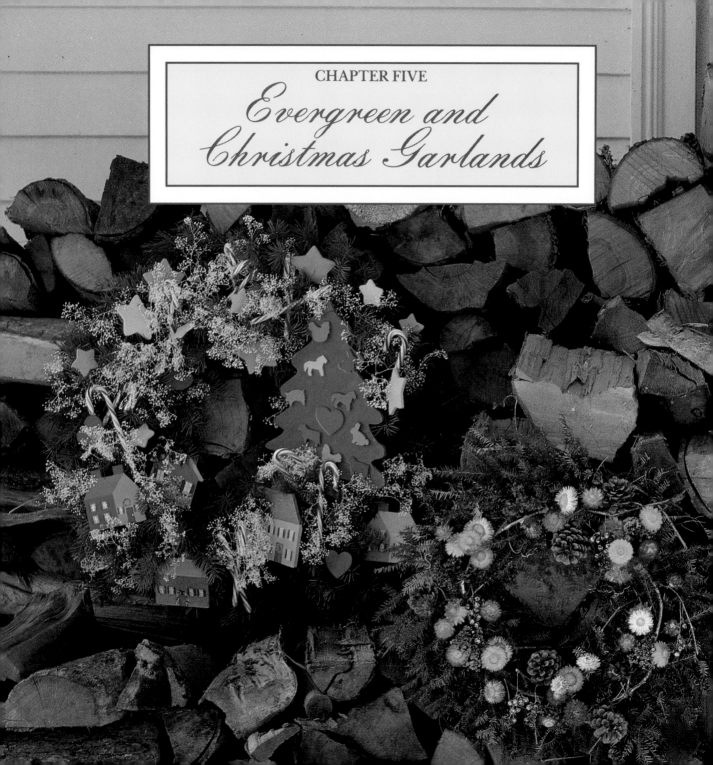

CHAPTER FIVE

Evergreen and Christmas Garlands

Traditionally, the Christmas season is the time when the garland takes a prominent stand. Evergreens abound and are used for their availability as well as their delightful aroma. Great red ribbons flow from the top of lush green garlands, and pinecones nestle in the boughs. It is always a pleasure to take drives through neighbourhoods to see the variations on this standard.

*T*he hunting horn placed within this evergreen garland repeats the circular form of the garland. Apples, wired and tucked into clusters of blue cedar berries, combine with ornamental gourds to evoke the traditional symbol of hospitality and welcome. Gold-sprayed magnolia leaves and pinecones extend the seasonal festiveness.

This garland could stand proudly as an outside decoration, or could be perfect for the entrance hall.

Not all Christmas garlands need an evergreen foundation to reflect the spirit of the season. A white-painted and glittered grapevine garland becomes the base for a collection of individual tuzzy-muzzies. Each little tuzzy-muzzy or nosegay is intended to be given as a gift after a party, as the guests are departing. Sprigs of herbs, a cinnamon stick, and dried flowers are first wired together with florist's wire, then covered with gold metallic ribbon, and finally collared with gold doilies. Gold balls and long stems of painted pods add to the overall design.

You can make the tuzzy-muzzies with fresh flowers, as is the tradition, but dried flowers and herbs allow more time to prepare the lovely take-home keepsakes. Wrap some of your gifts to match the colours chosen for your tuzzy-muzzies and decorate each package with a gold doily. Finally, insert the finished tuzzy-muzzies in the hollow open spaces of the vine garland, making sure that they are secure enough to hold but can still be removed without too much trouble or awkwardness.

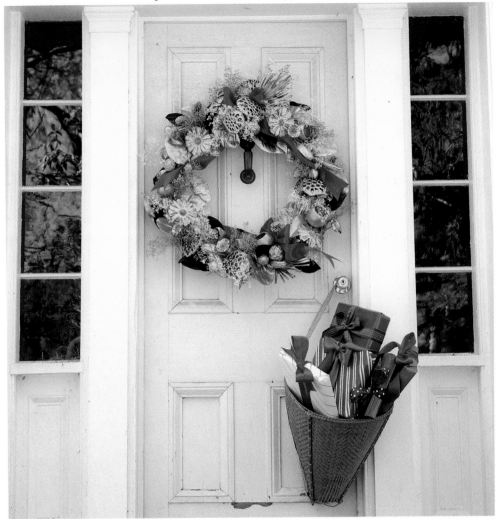

Another seasonal celebration is this gold-dipped vine garland filled with pods, cut palmetto, and sea-grape leaves also dipped in bright metallic gold. These festive materials are available through your local florist. Their brilliance simply sings out the joy of the season. Preserved green magnolia leaves and glittered baby's breath combine with great red satin ribbons to finish off the composition.

105

*U*sing the most contemporary of materials, this opalescent white sparkle garland captures the frosty, wintry feeling of the holiday season. Small packages wrapped in opalescent papers and stars, and branches treated with glitter and festive silver ribbon unite to form a full composition that brightens up a seasonal mantle or front door. Glittered white baby's breath, strands of opalescent beads, and small opalescent leaves add to the rich, sparkling texture. Most of the elements were simply glued into place with a hot-glue gun, while a few ornaments needed to be wired. The process is one of building up layers of textures and creating a density that becomes an allover volume of unified richness.

*T*his mantel ledge holds four wire-ring garlands, each treated individually. The corn garland was first covered with paper ribbon, wrapping the wire frame tightly. The big paper bow on the top was made by unrolling the coil of paper and securing it in place with a piece of wire. Corn was strung in loops, wrapped around the twisted paper, and then secured under the paper bow.

On another wire frame, this one made with a top hooklike clasp, sections of dried pineapple slices were strung. The garland was rehooked and a thin green ribbon was tied on top covering the mechanics.

The apple heart is made just like the dried pineapple garland. I straightened out the one side of the hooklike clasp with a pair of pliers and skewered the apples, pushing them to the other end of the frame. When the frame was full, I returned the hook to the clasp, locked the latch together with the other hook, and concealed the mechanics with a ribbon.

The berry garland is again on a wire frame. First cover the frame with small lengths of silver king, tying them onto the frame with lengths of florist wire. String the berries and twist the strands around the base to a desired fullness. Tie off the ends and place a small, thin ribbon bow on the side of the garland just for fun. These little garlands make wonderful holiday gifts. They are rather simple to construct, and it is something the whole family would enjoy doing together. Add them to your Christmas packages with a fresh sprig of holly or evergreen.

This brightly painted little village nestled under a great tree is made from pre-cut wooden shapes, all purchased through craft stores. The tree was cut by hand to conform to the scale of the garland. All the small animals on the tree were pre-cut and sold in a group. All the stars, the houses, and the great tree were hot-glued to six-inch florist's picks and inserted in the evergreen frame. Thirty-six candy canes were left in their wrappers, wired onto florist's picks, and placed around the garland. Lots of bright bleached baby's breath was used to simulate the snow and wonderland nature of the scene. In making a garland using wooden elements, remember to paint the pieces with water-base acrylic paint. It can stand up to the harsh winter weather if the garland is hung outdoors.

traditional evergreen garland rings in seasonal cheer with a cascade of brass bells emanating from a cluster of gold balls and larger brass bells. The gold metallic ribbon and strand of beads that wrap around the garland add to the texture of this festive creation. It is an easy way to dress up a purchased evergreen garland and at the same time create your own unique holiday statement. Substitute the bells with sprayed pinecones or Christmas-tree balls and you can achieve a similar look without the expense of the brass bells. It is not important that you have the same materials as illustrated in this book. Many substitutions work equally well.

This crab-apple-and-corn heart was executed on a wire frame that was first covered with boxwood—any seasonal evergreen would also work. Once the heart was wound with waxed twine the apples were put into place. First they were secured to florist's picks, then inserted into the evergreens. The tension of the wrapped evergreens along the wire frame is sufficient to hold the apples and picks. A garland of corn was wound around the heart and secured at the top of the heart. To hide the construction, as well as to enrich the festiveness of this welcoming heart, a red satin ribbon was tied to a bow with flowing ends. Another version of this heart could include small oranges, a lemon, a lime, or apples. If fruit isn't at hand, glue some nuts to florist's picks and use them.

This twig-and-evergreen heart actually consists of two different wire heart frames. The larger one holds the evergreens and was constructed by placing small amounts of fresh evergreen on the wire frame and winding them securely with waxed twine. The twig heart, with small decorative balls and red berries, was constructed in the same manner, but care was taken to add the balls and berries as the winding process developed. Both sides of the twig heart began at the lower point of the heart frame and worked up to the centre. There, a bow of two green ribbons and a cluster of multicoloured balls cover the construction.

115

This traditional fresh green garland with dried strawflowers and gold-sprayed dried grape clusters is made on a Polystyrene ring. The greens were wound with waxed twine. The strawflowers were inserted right into the Polystyrene, which holds each flower in place. A gilded strand of grapevine moves within the composition and carries out the feeling of freshness and country. Pinecones nest among the evergreen boughs, adding their own traditional presence.

116

*T*his garland made of large pieces of cinnamon glued onto a Polystyrene ring is an aromatic pleasure to have inside. Clusters of pomander, clove-filled oranges, a lime, and a lemon, each tied with gold cord, are gifts that can be removed, leaving a permanent garland of cinnamon sticks, pinecones, and silver king. The initial process takes some time and is best done with either designer tacky glue or a hot-glue gun.

inding an abundance of shells and pinecones, and drying some artichokes became the inspiration for this rather architecturally grand garland. Using a straw ring for the foundation, I hot-glued each shell and pinecone to four-inch florist's picks. The artichokes and a few selected shells and pinecones were lightly sprayed gold and attached with florist's picks. A handsome contrast between deep rich browns and shades of orange set off the white scallop shells. A gold-and-white cording stiffened with wire forms an articulated bow with a streamer that floats down among the shells.

*S*traw rings work very well as simple chandeliers for Christmas. Take a ring, measure the distance from the ceiling to where you wish it to hang, and cut to length three pieces of sturdy ribbon—red always comes to mind, but any colour would do. Allow enough ribbon to go around the straw ring and tie a secure knot. When you have tied three knots, and the balance of the garland has been adjusted, you may have to move the ribbon a little to the left or right until the garland floats parallel over the table. Then tie the three ribbon lengths together at the top and hang over a hook from the ceiling. Visit your local florist and purchase four plastic candleholders that have two long prongs coming from the base. Insert the prongs through the straw base. If they go all the way through, snip the ends off with a heavy-duty pair of wire cutters or garden shears. Make three separate bows from your ribbon and attach them at the junctions of each vertical ribbon support around the ring. Add any available fresh evergreens, and clusters of candy canes. Here I have also added some red berries. It is very important to remember that your evergreens must never be near the candles or they could burn.

Another possibility is to hang sweets or children's drawings with the candy canes. Cut out favourite Christmas-card pictures from past years and add them. It is really up to you to find what's just right for your home.

*T*his peppermint-candy garland is a great festive centrepiece and is also edible. Alternating stripes of wrapped peppermint candies and boxwood circle the Polystyrene form. A very easy way to make this centrepiece is to take three or four candies in their wrappers and wire them together with a two-inch florist's pick. The picks come with a wire attached. This process fills the spaces quickly, keeps the candy safe and clean in their wrappers, and doesn't require much effort or time. The boxwood is cut into short lengths and inserted directly into the Polystyrene. Add some metallic or plaid ribbon bows and fill the centre with tall taper candles in brass candlesticks, or circle the centrepiece with tiny votive candles in glass containers. Everyone will find this the sweetest of decorative garlands.

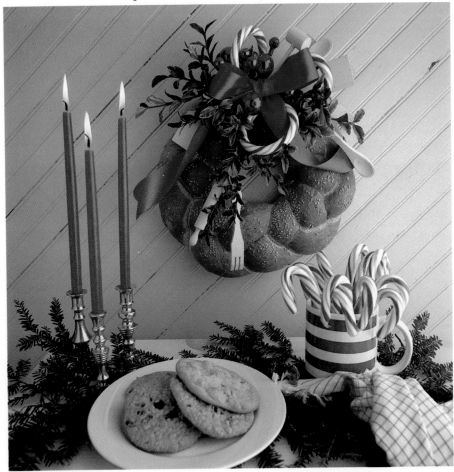

A real kitchen garland for Christmas is made out of a loaf of braided bread that has dried and become hard. To preserve it you should coat the whole loaf, top and bottom, with a clear acrylic spray. Add evergreens, peppermint-candy rings, and small wooden ornaments and balls. Simply insert each element directly into the bread. A hot-glue gun will ensure that they stay right where you desire. It is essential to wire the candy rings to a florist's pick. This is an easy decoration to make and would be a charming gift to give at this time.

You can always speed up the drying time by placing your loaf of bread in the oven. Set the temperature on low and leave the bread in until it feels totally hard and dry. Remember to give it a protective coating before decorating it.

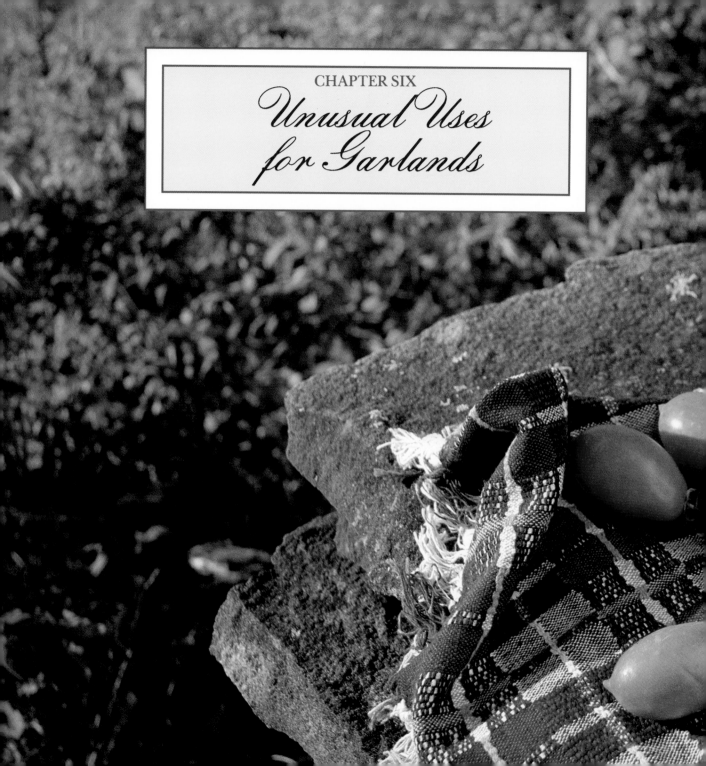

CHAPTER SIX
Unusual Uses for Garlands

*T*he uses of garlands and vines are as endless as your imagination. As well as being beautiful decorative pieces, garlands can be successfully incorporated into a wrapping or a presentation of a gift. The art of wrapping up a special jar of garden-grown tomatoes can be made even more special with a twist of grapevine. It is not difficult to do; just remember to lock each end of the vine into the body of the garland. Wrap a gold-sprayed vine garland around gifts from the kitchen and add fancy paper, or leave the vines natural and add a bit of your favourite fabric. Either way the recipient will be overjoyed by not only your gift but also your special way of presenting it.

A basket makes a perfect foundation for grapevines, because each vine can easily pass between the woven components of the basket structure. Here a vine covers the lower portion of a basket filled with moss and sprouting a beautiful bouquet of pears.

126

You can easily "countrify" your kitchen or bathroom by wrapping a vine garland around an apothecary's jar or a large jam jar. Fill one with soap for the guest bathroom or ornament one with strawflowers for the kitchen. During the Christmas season, make small garlands from evergreens and place them around decanters. With a little imagination and creativity, your skills at garlandmaking will be put to good use all year long.

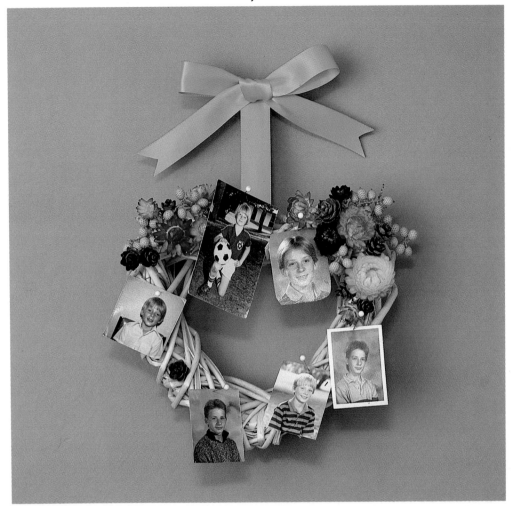

*E*very parent is proud of their child, and every grandparent or favourite aunt or uncle would enjoy a little garland filled with photographs. Here the standard school photograph becomes the collection, but any photograph would do. Add a few flowers and send it off to warm the hearts of relatives far away. Again, take advantage of the variety of ready-made bases, as their colours and materials will often inspire an idea or remind you of someone who would greatly appreciate receiving one.

*I*t seems there are always a few flowers left over when you make a big garland, a few extra pinecones and so on. The best way to use them up is to make a number of small garlands using any type of foundation. Make them and save them and then use one as an ornament for a special gift. The yellow package has a pre-made cinnamon heart on it with a raffia bow. A few extra strawflowers grace the bow and bring a little colour. The hearts come in three sizes and you will find a number of decorative uses for them. The mauve garland is also pre-made and comes painted. It has been decorated with mauve baby's breath and small flowers from a larger hydrangea blossom. The ribbon is a rich, deep burgundy, and the whole package has a subtle blending of similar colours. The bright little garland is made on a small straw base and is filled with a potpourri of coloured strawflowers, some very tiny pinecones, and a few sprigs of baby's breath. A bow using cornhusks has been made for the garland.

A Polystyrene base was covered with designer tacky glue and loose potpourri was pressed around the garland form. This sweet, fragrant garland has a few roses glued to the top and is anchored to the gift box by an apple-green satin ribbon.

The last gift is wrapped with brown paper and tied together with a length of fresh grapevine. This piece of vine retains clusters of dried grapes. Grapevines make wonderful package wraps, but it is important to securely lock both ends of the vine into the package.

$\mathcal{G}$arlands as centrepieces can be very beautiful. This bright zinnia garland has as its base a ring of oasis. Oasis is a material that when immersed in water retains the water for some time, keeping fresh flowers alive for many days.

In this example I took an oasis, wet it, and placed it on a large copper tray. With garden-picked flowers and sprigs of mint, rosemary, and sage, I've made a quick summer garland for the table. I find using fresh flowers throughout the growing season to be one very simple and easy way to decorate a table. Oasis rings come in a number of sizes and are available at your florist's.

*M*oss and spring flowers offer endless possibilities for creative seasonal garlands. Pansies, dusty miller, and freesia pop up through a rich covering of moss, celebrating the awakening of spring.

This garland was made entirely with fresh flowers placed in water tubes. The tubes were then attached to florist's picks and inserted into a moss-covered straw base.

135

When autumn rolls around and the fresh flowers become increasingly hard to find, it's good to go back to dried materials and the handy glue gun. This centrepiece was constructed from a piece of plywood.

Simply cut a circle and remove the centre, keeping an equal proportion for the ring. Drill four holes to fit standard candles. Hot-glue a variety of flowers, seed pods, and small pinecones to the plywood in a full, richly textured pattern of colours and forms. Because of its combination of appeal and beauty, this garland would look equally good on either a formal table or a country-kitchen pine.

Something a bit more casual but just as functional is this bread centrepiece. Protect the bread against moisture by using acrylic spray. Make sure to really coat it well to prevent the bread from turning after you apply your decorations.

Ornament the ring of bread with small clusters of strawflowers, eucalyptus, a few pieces of lichen and moss, and a couple hydrangeas, and finish it off with a few strategically placed candles.

$\mathcal{T}$hese three candle rings are simply three examples of an endless variety of solutions for the base of a three-inch candle. Two bases were cut from ³/₄-inch (2-centimetre) plywood and one is a wire ring. In making the wire ring I used the winding method to apply baby's breath and pinecones. It is an easy process and quickly makes a festive base.

The two wooden bases have a ribbon of woven fibre glued to the outer edge of the ring, and are finished off with a flat bow. Here, again, I used my trusty hot-glue gun to attach the ribbon to the wooden ring. The top of the ring surface is covered with sheet moss, with individual miniature pods glued into random clusters. Finally, I added tiny pinecones into the deep monochrome palette of the pods and moss. These little garlands are small, easy to make, and a good way to use up some left-over materials. However, if the candle is lit it should never be left unattended.

The garland in the foreground is on a wooden ring that is totally covered with moss. In this case, the moss covers the whole outer edge of the ring, eliminating the need for a ribbon. Strawflowers, bits of eucalyptus, and a few pieces of dried sage mix to form a rich, full garland.

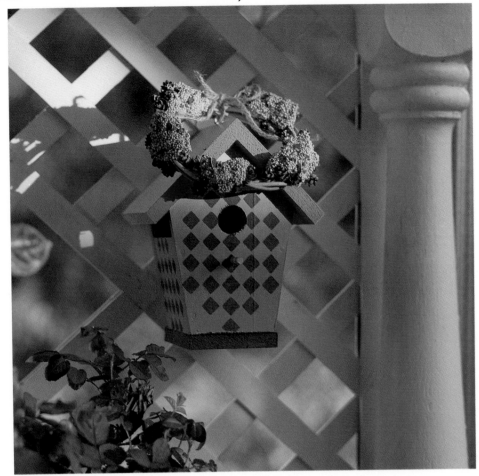

When the summer birds leave their homes, and the winter winds chill the air, it is time to make a few very special garlands just for the birds. This small grapevine garland that has been tied to the top of a painted birdhouse is filled with clusters of pinecones stuffed with peanut butter and a variety of seeds. I enjoy watching the birds eat from small garlands placed around the garden. You can easily hang them from tree limbs and from your porch. It is possible, of course, to make larger feeding garlands using combinations of standard winter feeding materials. Experiment and enjoy the challenge. I often include orange slices, grapes, corn, and berries, as well as oats and other summer grasses. The squirrels will also thank you for providing them with tasty treats.

This book has provided you with a great number of ideas as well as instructions for making your own garlands. The step-by-step procedures will help, as will the tips in finding or preserving flowers and pods. It is always recommended that you frequent your local florist, favourite craft shop, or garden centre and look for the familiar and unfamiliar materials that they carry. Don't be afraid to ask questions or to experiment with what you are working with. The more control you develop the richer your experiences will become, and the more pleasure you will derive from making garlands. I cannot stress enough that you should approach garlandmaking with an attitude that indeed you can do it and that you can freely interpret the way in which your garland develops. Be flexible, as that will bring you more rewarding pleasure and give you the best creative results. Mostly, I wish you the courage to try and satisfaction in having done so.

Sources

Most materials, tools, and other items mentioned throughout this book are available from your local craft shop, florist's shop, or DIY store. In the event of difficulty, however, the following details may be of assistance:

Hot Glue Guns and Other DIY Tools
All branches of W. H. Smith Do It All

Polystyrene Bases
The Handicraft Shop
Mail Order Department
Northgate
Canterbury CT1 1BE
0227-451188

Floral Art Scissors, Pocket Pruners, Wire Cutters, Florist's Tape
Flora Products Mail Order
(Stanley Gibbons Magazines, Ltd)
5 Parkside
Christchurch Road
Ringwood, Hampshire BH24 3SH
04254-2363

Pressed Flowers and Full Range of Cards
Impress
Slough Farm
Westhall
Halesworth
Suffolk IP19 8RN
098681 422

Ribbons and Additional Craft Materials
Pretty Things (Crafts) Ltd
7 Greenfield Road
Harbourne
Birmingham B17 OED
021 427 7433